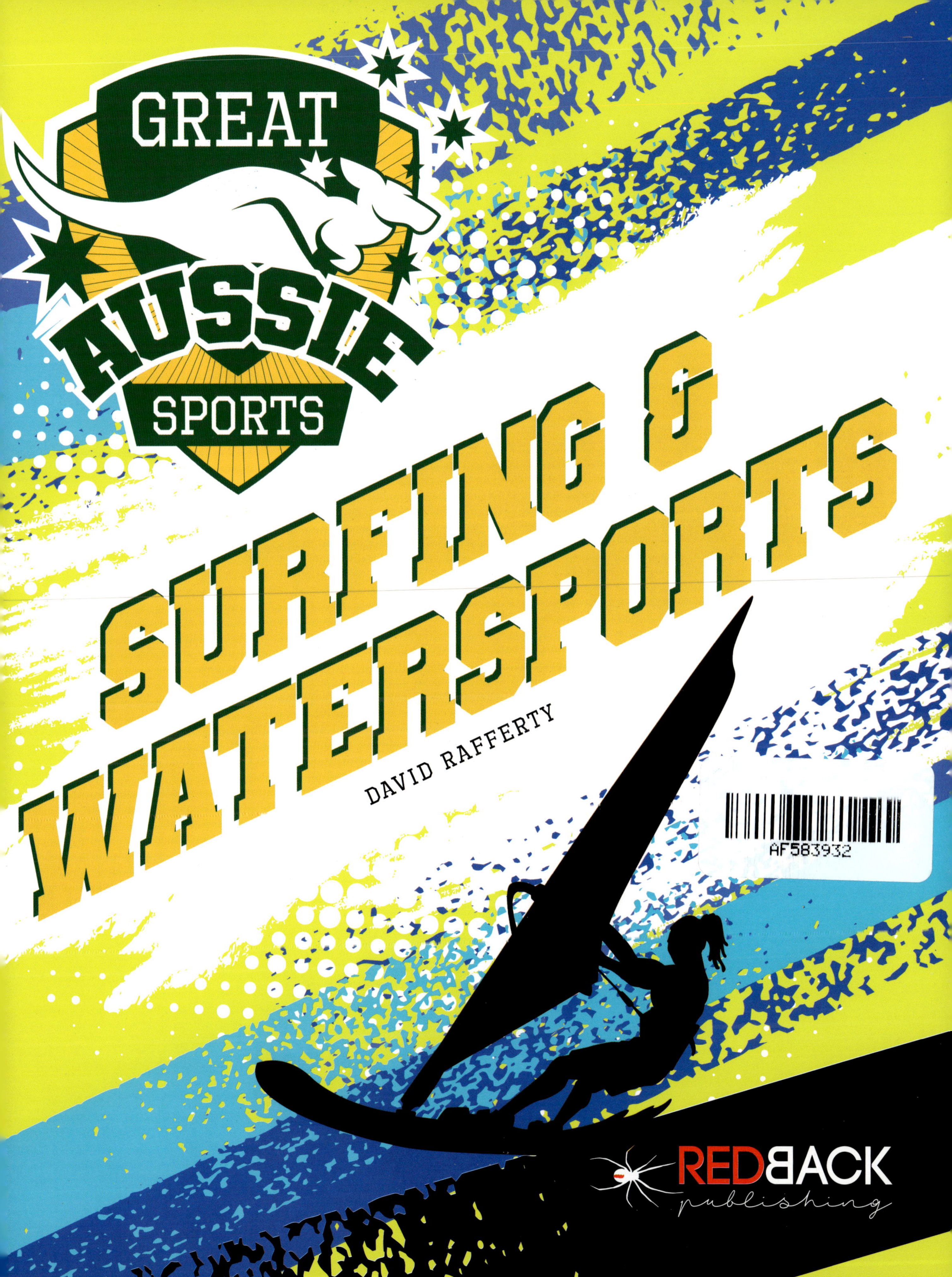

GREAT
AUSSIE
SPORTS
SURFING &
WATERSPORTS
DAVID RAFFERTY
AF583932
REDBACK
publishing

Redback Publishing
PO Box 357 Frenchs Forest NSW 2086
Australia

www.redbackpublishing.com.au
orders@redbackpublishing.com.au

978-1-925860-57-3 PBK

Author: David Rafferty
Editor: Caroline Thomas
Designer: Redback Publishing

A catalogue record for this book is available from the National Library of Australia

Original illustrations © Redback Publishing 2022
Originated by Redback Publishing
Printed and bound in Malaysia

Acknowledgements
Abbreviations: l—left, r—right, b—bottom, t—top, c—centre, m—middle
We would like to thank the following for permission to reproduce photographs: (Images © shutterstock)

p4t(r) Duke Kahanamoku c1912, by Jodi Rose / CC BY (https://creativecommons.org/ licenses/by/2.0), via Wikimedia Commons,
p4m Freshwater, Australia - March 03: sculpture of the first surfer - a memorial and landmark from the surfers area on Freshwater Beach on March 03, 2008 in Freshwater, New South Wales, Australia, by fritz16, via Shutterstock.com,
p7t Surfer paddling across a set of waves by bigwavephoto [Public domain], via Wikimedia Commons,
8b Peniche, Portugal - October 17 : Julian Wilson (AUS) during the Rip Curl Pro Portugal, October 17, 2013 in Peniche, Portugal, by homydesign, via Shutterstock.com,
9t Jeffreys Bay, South Africa - July 13, 2019: Stephanie Gilmore surfing during round 16 at the Corona Open J-Bay at Supertubes. A World Surf League championship event, by LouisLotterPhotography, via Shutterstock.com,
13t Barcelona - 22, Sept: Swimmers on the open waters event Crossing Travessia Barcelona Port on September 22, 2013 in Barcelona, Spain, by Maxisport, via Shutterstock.com
p14b Gold Coast, Australia - April 05, 2018 : Athlete swimming during 2018 Gold Coast Commonwealth Games at Gold Coast Aquatic Centre. By Abdul Razak Latif, via Shutterstock.com,
p15t 141100 - Siobhan Paton swimming - 3b - 2000 Sydney podium photo, courtesy of Australian Paralympic Committee / CC BY-SA (https://creativecommons.org/ licenses/by-sa/3.0), via Wikimedia Commons,
p15m Taipei/Taiwan - 13 December 2011: Wooden Olympic rings in exhibition room of national Olympic Committee. Creative way representing olympic rings by putting several pieces of wood together, by Tata Chen, via Shutterstock.com,
p15b Budapest, Hungary - Jul 30, 2017. Bronze medalist HORTON Mack (AUS) at the Victory Ceremony of the Men 1500m Freestyle. FINA Swimming World Championship. By katacarix, via Shutterstock.com,
p16t Budapest, Hungary - Jul 17, 2017. FORD George, australian waterpolo player. FINA Waterpolo World Championship was held in Alfred Hajos Swimming Centre in 2017, by katacarix, via Shutterstock.com,
p16b Mersin June 19:unidentified water polo players in action during the men. 17. Mediterranean Games match between Italy and France, final score 9 - 6. June 19 , 2013 in Mersin Turkey, by muratart, via Shutterstock.com,
p17t Kaposvar, Hungary - November 14: Gyenes (L) and Juhasz-Szelei in action at a Hungarian National Championship water-polo game (Kaposvar vs Kecskemet), November 14, 2009 in Kaposvar, Hungary, by muzsy, via Shutterstock.com,
p17b Kiel, Germany, 22 June 2019 - 125th Kiel Week. The 49th International canoe polo Kiel Week tournament at the keel line, by penofoto, via Shutterstock.com,
p18m Barcelona - Feb 17: Hungarian player Arpad Babay of CN Mataro in action during the Spanish kings cup 1/8's match against CN Monjuich in Sant Andreu swimming pool , February 17, 2012 in Barcelona, Spain, by Maxisport, via Shutterstock.com,
p19m Rio de Janeiro-Brazil, November 17, 2015- Women's Tournament of water polo. Brazil and Australia, by A.Ricardo, via Shutterstock.com,
p19b Rijeka, Croatia - January 21: water polo match between "Croatia" and "Russia" (water polo world league) 2009 in Rijeka, Croatia, by Lario Tus, via Shutterstock.com,
p21t 4high (show skiers), by Jonathunder / CC BY-SA (https://creativecommons.org licenses/by-sa/3.0), via Wikimedia Commons,
p23m Pacuare River, Costa Rica - March 14 2019: Kayakers fights the white water in the Pacuare River, Costa Rica, by Pafnuti, via Shutterstock.com,
p24b Banja Luka, Bosnia And Herzegovina - July 16: An unidentified athlete from Croatia competes at European Junior and U23 Canoe Slalom Championships on Jul 16, 2011 in Banja Luka, Bosnia and Herzegovina. The event is from July 14-17, 2011 by evronphoto, via Shutterstock.com,
p25tr 2017-07 Natural Games Playboating 103, by Antoine Lamielle / CC BY-SA (https://creativecommons.org/licenses/by-sa/4.0), via Wikimedia Commons,
p30t Hossegor, France - September 25: Sally Fitzgibbons wins the women's pro championship Roxy Pro september 25, 2013 in Hossegor, FRANCE, by peapop, via Shutterstock.com,
p30m Layne Beachley at the G'Day USA Penfolds Black Tie Icon Gala. Hyatt Regency Century Plaza, Los Angeles, CA. 01-13-07, by s_bukley, via Shutterstock.com,
p30br Peniche, Portugal. October 13 2013: Mick Fanning in the wave, during the Moche Rip Curl Pro Portugal, Supertubos beach, by Gaston Piccinetti, via Shutterstock.com,
p31b Biarritz, France - July 14: Stephanie Gilmore defeats Coco Ho during the first semi final at the women's pro championship Roxy Pro July 14, 2012 in Biarritz, France., by peapop, via Shutterstock.com,

CONTENTS

IN THE WATER

Australians participate in a wide range of watersports, from swimming to surfing and even underwater hockey. Each sport requires different skills and allows for varying levels of participation. Most watersports can be enjoyed by anyone with the willingness to learn and the right equipment. Some watersports, such as swimming and water polo, are enjoyed both recreationally and contested at the Olympics. You can find the level of any watersport that's right for you, from holiday camps for fun, to competing in the World Championships.

The Captain and the Duke

While in Hawaii, in 1788, Captain James Cook's lieutenant, James King, noticed his captain admiring the local surfers. He wrote in his journal that the surfers there seemed to feel 'a great pleasure' in the exercise. Hawaiian surfer and Olympic swimming champion, Duke Kahanamoku, introduced the sport to Australia in 1914 with a surfing demonstration at Freshwater Beach, north of Sydney. In 1994, a statue was erected at the beach in the Duke's honour, to recognise his contribution to surfing in Australia.

The Cost of Watersports

Some watersports can cost a lot of money while others can cost next to nothing. Swimming, for example, is a very cheap activity. Waterskiing on the other hand can be quite expensive because of the equipment involved.

Beach Culture

Australian beaches are among the best in the world, and for many Australians beach culture is a part of their national identity. Surfers flock to the beach when the waves are good. Swimmers, body boarders and body surfers share the shorelines with kitesurfers, windsurfers and stand-up paddleboarders.

Organised Watersports

Almost all watersports in Australia have organisations that govern the sport and run competitions. Joining a sporting organisation is a great way to meet other people who also enjoy the sport, and a good opportunity to get involved with fun community events and even participate in local and national competitions.

SURF SAFETY

Waves are what make surfing possible, make body boarding fun and ocean swimming exciting. Some beaches produce perfect surfing waves all year round. Other beaches, such as Victoria's famous Bells Beach, only provide surfing waves at certain times of the year.

Always Check the Weather

Ocean sports and activities take you into the wild, and put you at the mercy of Mother Nature. This can be extremely exhilarating and dangerous in equal measure. Always make sure to check the online surf report for the beach you're heading to before you set out. Check the weather forecast to make sure storms or winds aren't coming your way either.

Dumping Waves

One of the biggest risks faced by all types of board riders and ocean swimmers is being dumped by a big wave. Waves are very heavy and serious injuries can happen if the weight of the wave pushes you into the ocean floor. The important thing to remember when caught by a big wave is to keep your arms up above your head, to protect your neck and head as you go 'over the falls'. Once you are down and start to become pushed along by the wave, roll yourself into a ball to minimise the area of your body that the water can push against. Once the worst of the pushing has passed, open your body out wide again to regain flotation.

Close to Shore

On many beaches, particularly Australian beaches, good waves form no more than 50-100 metres from the shore. One advantage of close to shore activities is that the board rider or swimmer usually has a lot of company. This can be handy in case you get into difficulty. On some beaches, close to shore activities are supervised by Surf Life Saving clubs. The safest place for swimmers and body boarders is between the red and yellow flags. Surfers must stay outside these flagged swimming areas as their hard boards, with sharps fins below, can be dangerous to swimmers.

The Five Minute Rule

Experienced ocean sportspeople know that it takes at least five minutes to assess the water before taking the plunge. Ocean waves come in sets, with a distinct lull between each. By counting the number of waves in a set and timing the length of the lull, a swimmer or surfer can time both their entry and exit from the surf to either minimise their wave exposure - when going out for instance - or maximise it - when coming back in. Studying the surf before jumping in will also give you the time to notice where the rips are – the flat parts of the surf where the water flows back out to sea.

It's important to know where the rips are so that you can use or avoid them. Surfers and swimmers use rips to get out past the waves quickly. The rip is sometimes called a 'magic carpet' because the fast flowing water transports its occupant out to sea. Trying to return to shore through a rip is almost impossible and dangerous because it can cause extreme fatigue. Swimming against a rip is like swimming upstream in a river.

Submerged rocks, reefs and sandbars are other dangers. Surfers learn to 'read' the waves, watching for signs such as foamy patches or changes in the sea colour that might reveal what lies below. Even when all the signs are good, experienced surfers learn to accept their skill limits. Some waves are too big and too full for safe surfing.

Judging Waves

Seasoned surfers know what to expect from waves at a beach by studying them from the shore. Waves that cross a sudden trough in the seabed will tend to break too close together for good surfing. Other waves will fail to 'peak'– that is, develop full form before breaking. Waves that rise and peak in a regular series provide some of the best surfing. Some waves stretch unbroken for 50-100 metres, rising as high as two to three metres to form a hollow within the curve – or 'cave' – that a skilled surfer can speed along.

SURFING

In Australia, surfing can be enjoyed both for fun and as a competitive sport. Surfers who choose to compete in national and international tournaments often spend the entire year catching waves and travelling the professional circuit.

Starting Out

Learning to surf takes practice and persistence. Although it is possible to get the feel and balance required for surfing on dry land, real practice requires real waves. Surfing associations, such as Surfing Australia, the Australian Windsurfing Association and the Australian Bodyboard Association always emphasise the benefit of practising with experienced surfers. Each state has a State Surfing Association that provides tips and coaching.

All aspiring surfers should be strong swimmers!

Boards

Most surfers use a short **Malibu** board made of fibreglass, with two or three fins at the back underside. The Malibu board took over from the much longer boards used by the early surfers. The earliest boards were made of wood and could be up to three metres long – which is long when compared to the 1.2 metres of the modern Malibu board.

Which Board?

Some surfers prefer long boards because they offer a fast yet smooth ride. Malibu boards are best for competitive surfers because they are very easy to turn in the water and are good for performing tricks and flips. Body boarders can choose between competition boards and fun boards. Competition boards are very strong, which makes them fast. Fun boards have more flex which makes them safer for less experienced riders, but this flex does slow down the ride. Windsurfers change sails more than boards. Sails may be heavier for strong winds and lighter for soft winds.

Basic Surfing Moves

Start out by learning the basics of surfing, such as paddling, duck diving, popping up, and trimming. Once you can navigate a board safely out through the waves and back in again, it's fun to start adding more complex moves into your surfing session. Try these moves for starters:

- **Bottom Turn**
  The first turn on a wave after dropping in that allows you to channel speed and momentum in your chosen direction.
- **Carve**
  Change your line and direction in open areas of the waves by putting your weight and power on the board's rail and tracing an arc in the water.
- **Cutback**
  Transfer weight to the back heel and use the front foot to tilt the board from rail to rail so that the it traces an S-shape in the water. This slows the rider down to return them to the wave's power zone.

Advanced Surfing Skills

Once you have mastered the basics, it's time to test your skills. Competition surfers have a range of tricks to show off and professional surfers have their personal favourites. Here are just some of the more popular moves:

- **Snap or Slash**
  A complete change of direction while in the pocket or on the top of the wave that causes a showy spray of water.
- **Roundhouse Cutback**
  A figure-8 surf line performed in small waves without much wall that allows the surfer to return to the curl with increased speed and power.
- **Floater**
  Using speed to go over the top of a crumbling wave, then gliding horizontally over the top as it is about to break.
- **Tube or Barrel Ride**
  Riding the hollow part of the wave, fully covered by the curl's lip.

ENJOYING THE OCEAN

The ocean can be enjoyed in a number of ways, from swimming and surfing, to body boarding and bodysurfing. If waves aren't your thing, stand-up paddle boarding may be for you. If you prefer the thrill of mastering more complicated watercraft, kitesurfing and windsurfing are very popular in Australia. For very keen athletes, there are World Championships for most watersports.

Stand Up Paddle Boarding (SUP)

Stand up paddle boarding (SUP) involves the rider standing on the board, while using a paddle to propel themselves through the water. Sometimes this can be done as a variation of surfing, but stand up paddle boarders usually paddle on flat water. Some beaches don't have waves, while lakes or large rivers are also great places to SUP. In some areas, paddle board yoga has become popular.

Body Boarding

Body boarding is a version of surfing where the rider lies with their chest on a much shorter, wider and more **buoyant** board. The rider's hips and legs remain in the water, while their arms and hands steer by using a series of grip positions along the rails. Body boarders kick their legs and paddle with their arms to manoeuvre themselves onto waves. A **body board** doesn't have fins although hybrid boards may. Hybrids are shorter than surf boards, but longer than body boards and are usually made with the same materials as body boards. Body boards have a foam core with a soft top and a smooth plastic bottom. The soft top reduces the impact on the rider's body, while the smooth bottom allows speed in the water.

Bodysurfing

Bodysurfing requires the least equipment of any form of surfing. Bodysurfers use their own bodies like surfboards, taking off as a wave approaches and keeping the body straight with arms extended straight ahead. Because the human body is naturally buoyant, the water will speed a person along the wave. Movement is limited in bodysurfing and the speed is not fast, but it is still an exciting experience to catch a good wave. Best of all, the only equipment you need is your own body.

Kitesurfing

Kitesurfing combines the features of surfing, kite flying, paragliding and windsurfing. A kitesurfer uses a large kite (with five square metres of surface area) to pull his or her body along, while the feet are fixed into shoes (called grips) on the surface of a specially designed surfboard. Kitesurfers launch from the shore and use handles that are attached to the kite to harness the power of the wind. The kitesurfer is able to change direction, height and speed by moving the handles. The idea is to position the kite so that the rider can glide over the water on the board, ride waves and shoot up into the air. Kitesurfing competitions are becoming more common as the popularity of the sport grows.

If the wind is too powerful, there is a danger of being swept up too high into the air!

Windsurfing

With a sail attached to a specially designed surfboard, windsurfers are able to increase the speed at which they ride the waves. The surfer grips a flexible bar running across the sail, which is fixed into a socket in the surfboard. The rider can then angle the sail to control the direction of the board and perform tricks, such as becoming airborne. It is also possible to windsurf back up a wave after going down it. **Windsurfing** can be done on flat water or on waves, so long as there is a breeze.

SWIMMING

Australia has produced many swimming greats, from past champions Dawn Fraser and Ian Thorpe, to recent stars Leisel Jones and Ariarne Titmus. While Australians have won 186 Olympic swimming medals – more than in any other sport – for the everyday Australian, swimming is one of the most accessible sports. There are public swimming pools in most large towns and with many Australians living near the coast, ocean swimming can be exhilarating.

Fun and Recreation

Most swimmers enjoy the sport for the fun it offers and have no intention of making a career of swimming. But whether the aim of swimming is fun or elite-level competition, there is no doubt that many Australians have one thought in mind when the sun is out and a pool or beach is close by – jump in!

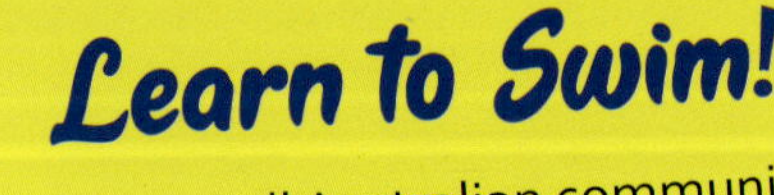

Learn to Swim!

Almost all Australian communities that have access to a pool, have learn to swim programs. Most local sports and recreation centres with pools offer swimming classes, and beginners can start as young as four months old. It is estimated that more Australian children either are or have been enrolled in swimming classes than in any other sporting program. One reason for this is the life saving benefits of the sport. With many Australians living near to water, swimming is considered an essential life skill.

Surf and Oceans Swims

Ocean swimming is a booming sport in Australia, with tens of thousands of swimmers participating in organised ocean and open water swimming competitions and races each year. Competitors may be newcomers to ocean racing, or world-famous professionals. One of the most famous surf swimming events is the Lorne Classic on the Victorian coast.

Helping Others

Surf Life Saving Australia enlists thousands of volunteers to help patrol beaches all along Australia's coastlines. Members of Surf Life Saving Australia are strong swimmers and have extensive knowledge of how to navigate challenging surf conditions. They are trained in first aid and can perform emergency rescues if a beachgoer gets into trouble in the surf. Volunteer surf life savers over the age of 16 must hold a Bronze Medallion Certification in Surf Life Saving. At age 14, keen swimmers can train for their Surf Rescue Certificate, to help patrol the beach as assistants to the Bronze Medallion holders.

SWIMMING COMPETITIVELY

Australia is one of the great competitive swimming nations of the world. Some of Australia's first Olympians were champion swimmers, and Australians have set records and brought home medals from international swimming tournaments for almost 100 years. Many communities have swimming clubs that compete in inter-club competitions. Joining a club as a junior might, with skill and dedicated training, open a path to competition that can lead all the way to the elite level.

Iron Men and Women

The Iron Man and Iron Woman titles are famous surf events. Competitors from Surf Life Saving clubs all over Australia, as well as professional Iron Man and Iron Woman athletes, take part in a series of surf swimming, surf ski and rescue board paddling events between January and March each year. The Australian Iron Man and Iron Woman are decided in the March events on a cumulative points system.

Serious Competition

If you want to swim competitively, you can start by joining a club, and racing other club members. This can help you to decide which events and swimming strokes suit you. If you wish to take swimming further, you can compete in championship events, racing swimmers from other clubs. At the next level, swimmers compete in State Championships and can then go on to compete in National Championships. National level swimmers may then compete internationally in such tournaments as the **Pan Pacific Championships**, the **World Swimming Championships**, the Commonwealth Games and the Olympic Games.

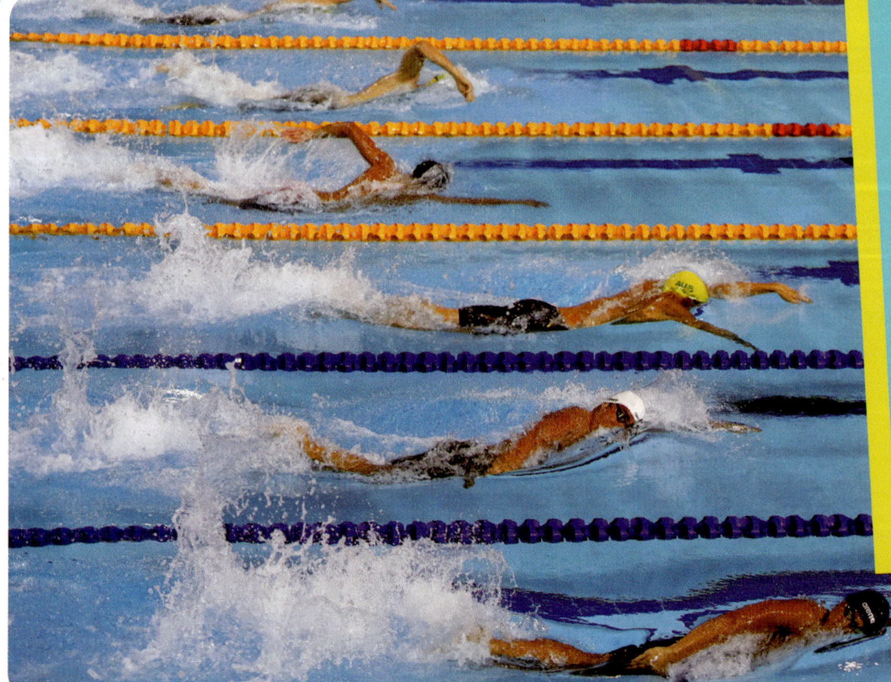

Paralympic Success

Australia's Paralympic swimmers have done exceptionally well in world competition. At the Sydney 2000 Olympics, Australian Paralympic swimmers won 14 gold, 15 silver and 21 bronze medals. The star was 17-year-old Siobhan Paton, who won six gold medals and broke eight world records. During the 2018 Gold Coast Commonwealth Games, the Paralympic races were integrated into the schedule, rather than being separated, and swimmers like Timothy Disken, Lakeisha Patterson and Brenden Hall won gold for Australia in front of cheering home crowds.

The Champs

Every decade produces a new group of Australian swimming champions. In the 1960s, champions such as Dawn Fraser, John and Ilse Konrads, Lorraine Crappe and Murray Rose were great Australian swimming stars. In the 1970s, Tracey Wickham and Shane Gould were at the top of the world. In recent times, Ian Thorpe, Grant Hackett and Susie O'Neill have set multiple world records and won gold at World Championships and at the Olympic Games. The latest set of swim stars includes Mack Horton, Mitch Larkin, the Campbell sisters – Bronte and Cate – Leisel Jones and Ariarne Titmus.

WATER POLO

Water polo has been played in Australia for more than 100 years, and Australians have regularly competed at international level. At the Sydney Olympic Games in 2000, the Australian Women's Water Polo Team won gold, scoring the winning goal with only one second left on the clock.

The Game

Water polo is one of the few team sports played in water. While swimming or treading water, players pass the ball to teammates with the objective of getting the ball into the opposing team's goal. Water polo combines features of rugby, ice hockey and basketball and is a very physically demanding sport.

Duration

A water polo match is played over four seven minute quarters. However, because the clock is stopped every time the referee blows the whistle, most quarters actually last at least 15 minutes. It is not uncommon for a match to last as long as 75 minutes. Players often cover up to three kilometres in the course of a game!

Serious Competition

Water polo was first played in Australia in the 1890s. By 1948, the Australian team had made it all the way to the Olympics. Today, National League teams from Sydney, Brisbane, Adelaide, Fremantle, Melbourne, Newcastle and Perth compete for the title of National Champion each year. Australian men's and women's teams are also regular competitors in the annual World Championships and in the World Cup which is held every two years.

Mixing it Up!

Water polo has been played in many formats over the years. Today, there are leagues around the world for variants of the game that include watercraft to help keep the players afloat. Some of these playing variations include:

- **Inner Tube Water Polo**
  Great for casual players, teams float in inner tubes while playing the standard game of water polo. This uses less energy and makes the game more accessible for different fitness levels.
- **Surfboard Water Polo**
  Duke Kahanamoku brought surfing to Australia, but his brother, Louis, introduced surfboard water polo to the world. Teams paddle surfboards while attempting toscore goals in the usual way.
- **Canoe Polo**
  Played in the World Games, teams paddle canoes while handling and 'batting' the ball into suspended goals. Tactics, speed and positional play are important.

Flippa Ball

Flippa ball is the junior version of water polo. The rules are modified to protect players from tackles that would be acceptable in the senior game and the player in possession is given much more freedom to pass the ball. Flippa ball is both an enjoyable and vigorous game and the ideal preparation for playing water polo.

Clothing

Players wear a swimming costume and a fabric cap with built-in ear protectors that ties under the chin. One side wears white caps, the other side, blue. The goalkeepers always wear red caps.

WATER POLO RULES

The rules of the game are designed to keep the game flowing while making sure that the play is fair. The Fédération Internationale de Natation Amateur (FINA) is the official governing body that overseas international competition.

The Teams

Each water polo team is made up of seven players. One player is the goalkeeper and the remaining six players both defend and attack. Players are free to move anywhere in the pool, as long as they do not take an offside position.

The Playing Area

Water polo is played either in a swimming pool or natural body of flat water with boundaries marked. FINA specifies that the regulation pool playing area for men's water polo should be 30 metres long by 20 metres wide and for women, 25 metres long by 20 metres wide. The depth of the water must be between 1.8 metres and two metres for both men and women. The junior version of water polo, known as **flippa ball**, requires a pool area 20 metres long by 15 metres wide. The goals consist of nets at each end of the playing area. They must be three metres wide and rise to a height of 90 centimetres above the surface of the water.

Passing

Players may catch the ball with one hand only and throw with one hand only. Once a team takes possession of the ball, the team has a maximum of 35 seconds in which to attempt a shot at goal. Within those 35 seconds, players may pass the ball to teammates as many times as they wish.

Offside

If a player other than the goalkeeper is within two metres of the goal at the same time as the ball, the player is said to be offside. This rule prevents players from blocking the goal, and prevents the side in possession from scoring too easily.

Scoring

The object of the game is to force the ball into the goals. This is usually accomplished by throwing the ball directly into the net, or by bouncing the ball off the surface of the water and then into the net. All goals are of equal value, no matter how they are scored. Any player may attempt to score.

Tackling

Water polo is a physical contact sport. Players may push, grab or attempt to stop a player who has the ball. However, players not in possession of the ball cannot be tackled. Tackling does not include striking another player. Tackling can be very fierce, but still legal. It is up to the referee to judge whether a tackle is too fierce. If the tackle seems designed to injure a player, the referee will award a free throw to the other side.

Fouls

There are two types of fouls in water polo, ordinary fouls and major fouls.

- **Ordinary Foul**
  Ordinary fouls can include a player impeding or shoving an opposing player who does not have the ball. Judged as less serious than a major foul, ordinary fouls are punished with an indirect free throw being awarded to the opposing side. A player cannot shoot for goal with an indirect free throw.

- **Major Foul**
  Holding another player, or sinking or pulling back an opposition player who does not have the ball is considered a major foul. The infringing player is removed from play and sent to the boundary of the pool for 20 seconds. If a major foul occurs inside the penalty area (within four metres of goal), the referee will award a penalty shot at goal to the opposing side. Only the goalkeeper may attempt to block the throw. If a player commits three major fouls in a game, he or she will be dismissed for the rest of the game, and must leave the pool.

Umpiring

Several officials work together to oversee a game of water polo. Two referees and two goal judges control the game from outside the pool. Table officials, including timekeepers and game secretaries oversee timings and record fouls and goals. The game referees, one on each side of the pool, walk up and down the length of the playing area, closely studying the game. They look for fouls committed not just above the water, but below the water as well. Goal judges patrol the goal areas to enforce the offside rules and to make sure that the ball actually passes the goalkeeper. The goal judges also keep watch on the shot clock, to make sure that a goal shot is taken within the legal time allowed.

WATERSKIING

Waterskiing is enjoyed by more people as a recreation than as a sport. Competitive waterskiing is exciting both to watch and to participate in. People attracted to the sport and wanting to participate or compete can join clubs where members share one or more boats.

Barefoot Skiing

A skiers feet, when on the right angle, can function as skis to keep the skier on the surface of the water. Because there are no skis, the skier can be closer to the boat and is more able to hear the driver. Barefoot skiing is a good way for beginners to learn before progressing onto skis.

Locations

Waterskiing demands a fairly smooth water surface, so lakes and rivers are the preferred locations for skiing. While it still might be fun to ski off-shore on the ocean, the swelling waves and ocean 'chop' reduce the speed at which the boat can travel and make the skier's task more difficult.

High Speed Boats

Waterskiing depends on a boat being able to build up high speeds. Before 1930, few boats were able to travel fast enough to pull a skier. Ted Parker, of Sydney, became the first Australian to waterski in Australian waters when he displayed his skill on Sydney Harbour in 1934. Waterskiing grew in popularity in Australia in the 1950s, when outboard motors and new techniques in making speedboats brought the price of boats down considerably.

Ski Racing

Skiers can reach speeds of 160 kilometres per hour and racing is an exhilarating sport. Competitors race over a three to four kilometre course, with the skier signalling the driver of the boat to go faster or slower.

Competitive Waterskiing

Skiers show their skills in **slalom**, jumping and trick events. Waterskiers compete in four forms of the sport:

- **Tournament Skiing**
  The most popular competitive event, with the longest competitive history.
- **Barefoot Skiing**
  In the absence of a ski, higher speeds are required to maintain lift. A barefoot skier usually wears a wetsuit so that they can speed along on their back until sufficient speed allows them to stand.
- **Ski Racing**
  Australia holds some of the world's longest and fastest ski races. Skiers compete in pairs around circuits or on long rivers.
- **Show Skiing**
  Elaborate costumes, choreography, and music usually accompany skiers in ski show events. Skiers form pyramids, perform double skiing acts, freestyle jumps and swivel skiing.

World Championship

Australia, the USA and Canada are the main countries that compete in international waterskiing. The World Championship is held every two years with participating nations hosting the tournament in rotation.

Tournament Skiing

Tournament water skiing consists of three events: the slalom, jumps and tricks.

The slalom calls for skiers to weave in and out of **buoys** floating on the water's surface. In the jumping event, skiers build up speed on the water before riding up a floating ramp and launching themselves into the air. They must then retain balance when landing at speed, back on the water. The tricks event demands the greatest skill of all with somersaulting, skiing backwards and turning 360° at high speed. Skiers are judged on the degree of difficulty involved in successfully performing their tricks.

CANOEING AND KAYAKING

The canoe and the **kayak** are based on simple types of boats, used for thousands of years for hunting, fishing and warfare. The canoe originates with the native Americans of North America, and the kayak with the **Inuit** and **Aleut** people of Canada and the Arctic. Today, both the canoe and the kayak are more widely used in the sports of canoeing and kayaking than in hunting and fishing. Canoeing and kayaking are Olympic sports, and both are popular in Australia.

The Boats

The **canoe** and the kayak are two versions of the one type of boat. A canoe is open at the top, like a rowboat, while a kayak is enclosed except for an opening that the paddler sits in. The other important difference is that when canoeing the paddle only has an oar on one side. The paddler uses the oar first on one side of the canoe, then the other. The kayak paddle has an oar on both ends. The paddler tilts the paddle left and right with alternate strokes. In professional canoeing, the paddler rests on his or her knees. In a kayak, the paddler is seated. In Australia, the term canoeing is often used for both canoeing and kayaking.

Both canoes and kayaks can be paddled by more than one person. In competition, one, two, three or four people can paddle. One-person kayaks are referred to as K1s, two person kayaks are called K2s, and so on up to K4s. One-person canoes are called C1s, up to C4s. Modern canoes and kayaks are made from fibreglass and plastic.

Safety First

The first requirement for anyone wanting to canoe or kayak is to be able to swim. The boats can capsize easily and it is essential to wear a life jacket whenever the boat is on the water. In whitewater, helmets should also be worn to protect paddlers in case the boat capsizes near rocks.

Paddle Your Own Canoe

There are many boat rental shops that hire out a variety of watercraft in most tourist destinations around Australia. Renting a boat for a few hours can give you a good idea of whether you may wish to pursue the sport on a more regular basis. If you find you enjoy the experience, canoeing and kayaking clubs are found in all the major Australian coastal cities and towns. Clubs are a great way to meet others who enjoy the sport and can sometimes offer more long term boat hire or shared ownership. Owning your own boat provides more flexibility, but does require additional consideration in terms of transportation.

Canoeing and Kayaking for Pleasure

Most kayakers and canoers do not compete, but the majority do belong to clubs and organisations that promote the sport. In terms of exercise, kayaking and canoeing are amongst the best recreations for developing aerobic fitness. Clubs organise outings to famous water sites, such as the King and Franklin Rivers in Tasmania, where members 'take it easy', enjoying the natural environment as much as the exercise.

CANOEING AND KAYAKING COMPETITIONS

In partnership with the Australian Sports Commission, Paddle Australia has an association in every state and territory – except the Northern territory. These associations oversee paddle competitions and events, and provide education and skills development pathways for beginners, right up to Olympic entry for elite athletes.

At the Olympics

Canoeing was showcased as a demonstration sport at the Paris Olympics in 1924. The canoe sprint event was included as an Olympic sport for the first time in 1936. One of the most difficult tasks for the country hosting the Olympics is to set out a course for the fast-water events, such as the slalom. Not all countries have natural waterways that can be used for slalom, so artificial courses have to be built, or rivers modified.

Marathon

The canoe or kayak marathon is a great challenge and calls for a high level of fitness. Competitors cover between 38 and 42 kilometres on both flat water and whitewater. In some marathons, the competitors remain in their boats for the entire journey. In other marathons, competitors must leave the water at certain points to carry the canoe or kayak overland, before returning to the water to complete the course.

Sprint Racing

Canoe sprint racing is one of the best known competitive canoeing disciplines. Boats have evolved to be sleek, fast and unstable. Paddlers race on flat water over distances of 200, 500 and 1000 metres.

Slalom

Slalom races run over approximately eight kilometres downhill, through gates that are set along a course which follows the current of a river or artificial waterway. Competitors must manoeuvre their boats through each of the gates at high speed. If a competitor misses a gate, they must paddle upstream against the current to ensure they go through the missed gate. Touching a gate incurs a two second penalty, while missing a gate incurs a 50 second penalty. Capsizing is always a danger in wild water and slalom events.

Canoe Freestyle

Canoe freestyle involves a whitewater paddler performing a range of acrobatic tricks such as spins, flips and turns similar to those seen from freestyle snowboarders, surfers and skaters. There are up to 30 different moves, many of which involve being airborne.

Ocean Racing

Canoe ocean racing includes long distance surfski, sea kayak and sea touring races. A surfski is the fastest boat over long distances on ocean swells. Racers can face large waves, challenging swells and strong winds.

Wildwater Racing

Wildwater canoe and kayak racing is very physically demanding. Boats are long and narrow with a rounded hull. This makes them fast but also unstable and hard to turn. Paddlers must use their body to tilt the longer boat to turn it, as the usual wide paddle stroke becomes ineffective. Wildwater canoeing is a timed event of either a long distance course or a short sprint.

WHITEWATER RAFTING

Whitewater rafting requires wild waterways, usually found in the mountains. Queensland, New South Wales and Tasmania have great rivers that are perfect for this sport, as does New Zealand. Further afield, the USA, Canada, South America and South East Asia attract thousands of whitewater rafters each year.

Whitewater Lingo

Crew must be familiar with the language of white watering, so that the guide's instructions are quickly understood. Some terms include:

- **Cartwheeling**
  Allowing the boat to turn in circles in a whirlpool
- **Eskimo roll**
  Getting the boat upright after a capsize
- **Eddy turn**
  Taking to the quiet water at the streams edge for a breather
- **Ferry**
  Crossing the river while facing upstream

Boat or Raft?

There are many types of **whitewater rafting**, ranging from extreme descents along raging **torrents** to skilled paddling down fast streams. Experienced paddlers can navigate rapids in specially designed kayaks, or teams of paddlers, from beginner to elite, can paddle **inflatable rafts.**

Rafting as a Team

Rapids are rated on an international scale of I to VI (1 to 6), with I being the least dangerous and VI being the most dangerous. Whitewater rafting requires input from every person in the boat. Each crew member must be ready to follow the leader's or guide's instructions quickly and confidently. The guide will call out, 'Dig!' when the crew are required to paddle strongly, or 'Ship!' when it is necessary to pull the oars into the boat and hold on while the raft is taken by a wild stretch of water. Each paddler is equipped with a safety helmet and life jacket, and sometimes knee guards. A wetsuit is essential protection against both cold and injury from submerged rocks if the boat capsizes.

10 OF THE BEST

Whitewatering is enjoyed all over the world, and some of the most thrilling rides are outside Australia. Ten great river rapids are:

- **Futaleufu River**
  Chile
- **Cherry Creek**
  California, USA
- **Zambesi River**
  Zimbabwe
- **Great bend of the Yangtze River**
  China
- **Rio Upano**
  Ecuador
- **Magpie River**
  Quebec, Canada
- **Karnali River**
  Nepal
- **Gauley River**
  West Virginia, USA
- **Salmon River**
  Idaho, USA
- **Nile River**
  Uganda

Kayaking on Whitewater

There are many obstacles in whitewater that the kayaker must avoid, so quick, skilful manoeuvring is essential. Paddlers can make the switch from flat water to whitewater by upskilling in a pool first, then testing skills gradually on whitewater. Helmets, life jackets, waterproof gloves, float bags (to hold onto after a capsize), ropes, dry clothing in a waterproof bag, and boots are essential for any trip.

INTO THE DEEP

Being under the water, instead of on top, provides a whole new world of possibilities.

Scuba Diving

The **SCUBA tank** (Self-Contained Underwater Breathing Apparatus), was invented in the 1920s. For the first time, prolonged underwater swimming and exploration became possible, and a whole new world of appreciation for our oceans and aquatic environments came with it. Thousands of Australians now enjoy the experience of exploring underwater for fun, for education and for science.

Strict Standards

Scuba diving in Australia is governed by the **Australian Underwater Federation** (AUF). Scuba diving instructors and clubs are required to meet strict safety regulations and display a very high level of technical ability in order to keep their AUF rating. All dive information is strictly recorded and equipment is tested regularly to constantly improve scuba diving safety standards.

Dive Safety

Scuba diving requires hours of training, and safety precautions are extensive and essential. A scuba tank is a specialised piece of equipment. Filled with compressed oxygen, it allows a diver to 'breathe' underwater for an hour or more when used correctly and safely. Special weights are attached to the divers belt to match their body weight and oxygen tank. This allows them to remain submerged. Flexible flippers provide speed and manoeuvrability in the water, and mist-free facemasks and rubberised wetsuits make the experience comfortable.

The Snorkel

A snorkel is a breathing tube that fits into the mouth at one end, while the other end can remain above the water. It allows a swimmer to breathe normally while their face is submerged in water. With a facemask and flippers, snorkellers can swim naturally while watching underwater life for hours. Alternatively, the snorkel can be used together with short dives in team sports, such as underwater hockey or underwater rugby.

Snorkelling

The Australian coast is one of the finest for enjoying **snorkelling,** with its countless coral reefs and rockpools. Wildlife isn't the only thrill of the underwater world. Australia also has stunning rock formations and even shipwrecks!

Underwater Hockey

In **underwater hockey** (or Octopush) players wear snorkels to swim down and manoeuvre a puck on the pool floor, with a 25 centimetre long wooden bat. Six players on each side attempt to push the puck through goals at each end of the pool. In addition to the snorkels, the players wear facemasks and flippers.

SURFING GREATS

Surfing World Championship

The Surfing World Championship is competed over a year-long series of events. Points are awarded for placement in each event and accumulate over the year. The male and female competitor with the greatest number of points become World Champions. Events are held at famous surfing beaches in Australia, the Pacific region and the Americas. The final event of the World Championship is the Rip Curl Surf Cup held at Sunset Beach in Hawaii in December each year.

SURFER PROFILE

LAYNE BEACHLEY

DATE OF BIRTH: SYDNEY, 24 MAY 1972

YEARS ON THE PROFESSIONAL SURFING CIRCUIT: 13

HIGHEST WORLD RATING: NO. 1 (1998, 1999, 2000, 2001, 2002, 2006)

FAVOURITE SURFING MANOEUVRES: ROUNDHOUSE CUTBACKS, FLOATERS, FOREHAND SNAPS

CAREER HIGHLIGHTS

- 7 X WORLD CHAMPION 1998, 1999, 2000, 2001, 2002, 2003, 2006
- 2005 LAUREUS WORLD ALTERNATIVE SPORTSPERSON OF THE YEAR AWARD
- 2006 SURFERS' HALL OF FAME
- 2011 AUSTRALIAN SPORTS HALL OF FAME
- 2015 OFFICER OF THE ORDER OF AUSTRALIA

SURFER PROFILE

MICK FANNING

DATE OF BIRTH: SYDNEY, 13 JUNE 1981

YEARS ON THE PROFESSIONAL SURFING CIRCUIT: 16

HIGHEST WORLD RATING: NO. 1 (2007, 2009, 2013)

FAVOURITE SURFING MANOEUVRES: HACKS AND TUBES

CAREER HIGHLIGHTS

- 3 X WORLD CHAMPION 2007, 2009, 2013
- 6 X AUSTRALIAN MALE SURFER OF THE YEAR 2002, 2004, 2007, 2008, 2010, 2011
- IN 2015, FANNING SURVIVED A SHARK ATTACK ON LIVE TELEVISION, WHILE COMPETING IN THE J-BAY OPEN 2015 FINALS AT JEFFREYS BAY, SOUTH AFRICA

GLOSSARY

Aleut the arctic-dwelling people of far northern Asia, who were once known as Eskimos

Australian Underwater Federation (AUF) a national organisation that regulates scuba diving and snorkelling in Australia

buoyant able to float

buoys anchored floating markers

canoe a long, narrow boat for one to four people, open on the topside, propelled with a single oared paddle

capsize to turn a boat over on its side

flippa ball a version of water polo for junior competitors, with modified rules

inflatable raft a boat that is collapsible, and which can be inflated by pumping air into its sealed, waterproof structure

Inuit the arctic-dwelling people of northern Canada and Greenland who were once known as Eskimos

kayak a long, narrow boat for one to four people, with an enclosed top, propelled with a double oared paddle

kitesurfing a form of surfing that involves the surfer holding a large, airborne kite while his or her feet are strapped to a special surfboard

Malibu board a short surfboard of approximately 1.2 metres

Pan Pacific Championships a swimming tournament held every two years, open to participants from nations bordering the Pacific Ocean

scuba diving underwater swimming with the aid of a scuba tank, face mask and flippers

scuba tank tank containing compressed oxygen used by scuba divers

slalom a race along a zigzag course defined by gates or poles

snorkelling breathing through a plastic tube while swimming with the face submerged

torrents rapid spills of water in a river or creek

underwater hockey a version of hockey played on the base of a swimming pool

water polo a team watersport with seven players per side, played in a swimming pool or on outdoor waters with set boundaries

whitewater fast-moving water in rivers and creeks

whitewater rafting rapid downstream boating on fast water in an inflatable raft

windsurfing surfing with a sail attached to a special surfboard

World Swimming Championships an international swimming tournament for all nations, held every two years

INDEX